D1523933

It's All Grace

How God's Grace Impacts Every Area of Life

Joseph Cosentino

CONTENTS

ACKNOWLEDGMENTS

To my wife, Melinda, who is a constant manifestation of God's grace
in my life.
To my son, Joe Jr., whose vision for me to have an office at home
provided the setting and inspiration to write this book.
To my daughter, Marianne Bulgrin, who did a wonderful job as
editor.
To my secretary, Rachel Zachardy, who had the dubious role of
reading my hand written manuscript and did an admirable job putting
it into type written form.
To the Men of the Word at Canton Grace, whose enthusiasm and
anticipation for this book kept me enthused throughout the process.
To Mariah Kovac whose wonderful artistic talent is displayed on the
book cover.
Without the help and encouragement of each of you, this book
would not have been possible.

Introduction: The Purpose of This Book

God's grace is truly amazing. It's His grace that keeps us breathing. It's His grace that grants us access to heaven. By His grace, we are the recipients of every good thing that we enjoy in this life. Nothing thrills my soul, creates wonder in my thoughts, or melts my heart more than meditating upon His grace.

Yet it's easy to go an entire day, if not week, without thinking about His grace. It's my goal to help each of us become more appreciative of God's grace in our own lives. I have chosen seven main areas of life to show how the grace of God impacts and enriches each area. I have purposefully used stories from my own life to illustrate God's grace. God's Word, which God has promised to richly bless, is also cited with frequency.

It is my hope and prayer that God will use this book to increase your love for the Lord Jesus, who makes all grace possible, and that you will regularly praise Him for His grace that He extends to you.

"And of His fullness we have all received, and grace for grace. For the law was given through Moses, but grace and truth came through Jesus Christ" (John 1:16-17).

Chapter One – God's Grace Growing Up

There are few variables in life that impact who we become more than our background. God weaves our genetic makeup, parental influence, siblings, friends, neighborhood, relatives, teachers, hobbies, and life changing events to build the foundation of who we will eventually become. From a human perspective, it is a mind boggling accumulation of variables that happen haphazardly. From God's perspective, it is a well-orchestrated symphony arranged to make you who you are. There are no accidents with God.

Boy Meets Girl

The marvel of who I am today starts in my finite mind with my parents, their upbringing, and how they met. My father was born in Italy in October 1929. He was raised without a father. His father was in the United States working to earn and save enough money to bring his wife, son, and three daughters to start a new life in the United States. My father barely knew my grandfather until he emigrated from Italy as a 17 year old. As you can imagine, being raised by his mother during World War II in detestable conditions affected who my dad became as an adult.

My mother is also of Italian descent. She grew up in Pittsburgh, Pennsylvania. She was the oldest of four very beautiful girls. The Cicero girls were known in Pittsburgh for their beauty as I discovered in my young adult life. My grandfather owned a gas station. As a result, my mother was well acquainted with the stress and unique challenges of a sole proprietor. This became an asset later when my father opened 'Joe Cosentino Custom Tailor.'

God's sovereign grace was on display when dad's family settled in Pittsburgh where my mother resided. His grace was magnified when my parents "just happened" to be at the same public pool on a hot summer day. My aunts and my mother's cousin were playing keep away with my mom's bathing suit cap. The cap was tossed in the water away from my mother. Dad sensing his opportunity, jumped in, retrieved the cap, and gave it to mom. I'm pretty sure that he had his eye on the fair maiden before he rescued her cap on her behalf!

What if dad had not gone to the pool that day? What if mom had stayed home? No chance. God, in His sovereign grace, arranged the meeting before time began. Frequently the little daily choices that we make alter our lives and the lives of others. Fortunately, God providentially controls those choices for His good pleasure. Proverbs 16:9 says, "A man's heart plans his way, But the Lord directs his steps." Solomon also writes in Proverbs 19:21, "There are many plans in a man's heart, nevertheless the Lord's counsel – that will stand." In Proverbs 20:24 we read, "A man's steps are of the Lord; how then can a man understand his own way?"

Our Parents' Backgrounds

My parents' backgrounds profoundly affected the people they became, which of course had a significant impact upon me as well. Growing up in Italy in World War II influenced my father his whole life. One of the positive influences was that his humble beginnings drove him to work diligently and with excellence. Dad made sure that he provided for his family and that we would never lack anything necessary. As a custom tailor, excellence and precision were the pillars of his craft. His life example pounded those two words into the core of my being. That is another outpouring of God's grace in my life. As a pastor and especially as a Bible teacher, excellence and precision are essential. As Paul noted, "Be diligent to present yourself approved to God, a worker who does not need to be ashamed, rightly dividing the word of truth" (II Timothy 2:15). By God's grace, we emulate numerous virtues that we observe in our parents.

My mother grew up in a typical warm, close-knit Italian family. She created the same welcoming environment when she became a wife and mother. My brother's Marc, Gino, and I all have friends who commented on the love and acceptance that they felt when visiting our house. Our friends would mention this decades after our teenage years. It was God's grace to grow up in that environment, but also to know how to help create that sense of community years later as a pastor with my wife Melinda.

There is one other aspect of my mother's life that points to God's grace. Mom was the great woman behind the highly successful man. Dad was widely recognized as the best custom tailor in

Pittsburgh. Dozens of my dad's customers told me that as I was growing up. Dad would have never lived the American dream without mom. She was dad's secretary, treasurer, sounding board, and financial advisor. I think of Proverbs 12:4 when I think of her, "An excellent wife is the crown of her husband, but she who causes shame is like rottenness in his bones."

It was God's grace to have a mother who made her husband look as good as possible, be as successful as possible, and grace his life in as many ways as possible. I was determined to find someone who would partner with me in the same way. I found her and she has been making me look good ever since.

My parents were also responsible for raising my two fine younger brothers, Marc and Gino. We had a tremendous amount of fun growing up. They were excellent younger brothers, who eventually followed me in giving their lives to Jesus Christ. Growing up in a quality family is another manifestation of God's grace.

Divine Protection – The Ultimate Body Guard

When we get to heaven, I imagine that we will become aware of countless times that the good Lord protected our lives. The protection likely will come in many different forms. It will be physical, spiritual, relational, vocational, and emotional in nature. The aspect of God's protection that we see most clearly in this life is physical.

One of my favorite passages in the Scriptures about divine protection is Psalm 121, "I will lift up my eyes to the hills- from whence comes my help? My help comes from the Lord, who made heaven and earth. He will not allow your foot to be moved; He who keeps you will not slumber. Behold, He who keeps Israel shall neither slumber nor sleep. The Lord is your keeper; The Lord is your shade at your right hand. The sun shall not strike you by day, nor the moon by night. The Lord shall preserve you from all evil; He shall preserve your soul. The Lord shall preserve your going out and your coming in from this time forth, and even forevermore."

In verses 1 and 2, the Psalmist identifies the source of our protection. The hills can provide a small measure of protection, but ultimately all protection comes from the Lord, the One who made the heavens and the earth, the Creator of the universe. He has the power to protect us from all danger. In verses 3 and 4 the strength of our divine protection is explained. God will prevent us from experiencing the slightest slip and is never too tired to be on duty. The Psalmist concludes by elucidating the scope of our protection.

He is always near, always on the job day and night, in every kind of danger, for as long as we live.

In Psalm 18:2, King David uses a string of names that all picture God's protective hand. "The Lord is my rock and my fortress and my deliverer; My God, my strength, in whom I will trust; my shield and the horn of my salvation, my stronghold."

I experienced God's protective hand growing up. Two short stories that took place a few months apart as an eleven year old illustrate how God protected me as a youngster.

One day in the summer of 1967, I was playing baseball for my Little League team, the Athletics. I came to bat early in the game and hit a long home run over the right field fence. I must have been overly anxious to hit again. Only one hitter was permitted to be loosening up to hit, the next batter. It was a well-rehearsed team rule. I got off the bench before the next batter walked to the plate to hit. While he was still warming up to hit, I came up behind him and he accidently hit me in the head with a practice swing. A knot on my head appeared immediately. My mother rushed me to the emergency room. The doctor greeted her with the good news, I was going to be fine. The sobering bottom line was the bat connected with my head less than ½ an inch from my temple. Sometimes God's grace can be measured in less than an inch.

A few months later in the fall of that year, I was playing touch football with some of my friends on the street. I suddenly heard a sound, turned around, and was instantly hit by a motorcycle. I flew straight up in the air, did a somersault, and landed on my feet. The only evidence that I had been hit by a motorcycle was that the sleeve of my short sleeve sweatshirt was slightly torn. My saving grace was that I was hit by one of the handlebars on the motorcycle and not the front tire. Less than one foot was the difference between an acrobatic moment and a severe injury.

Parental Guidance

Decisions that parents make are often pivotal in our development. The choices that parents make about where we live, if we are disciplined, and what interests we pursue strongly influence who we become.

Academically, I kept improving as my years in school progressed. I earned better grades in college than I did in high school and better grades in seminary than in college.

The decisive moment in my academic career took place at the end of my sophomore year in high school. I had been seriously distracted that year by my intense interest in baseball and the young ladies at Penn Hills High School. These two distractions contributed to a final report card that did not reflect my God-given abilities. My mother was well aware of my significant underachievement, so she "hit me" where it hurt the most. There would be no baseball next year if my grades did not improve to her satisfaction. The tone of her voice and the expression on her face let me know that she was dead serious. My grades were never a problem again as I applied myself to the academic task at hand. I thank God for a mother who knew how to motivate me to live up to my God-given potential.

My parents also knew which interests to encourage and which to ignore. Parents today seem intent upon letting their children try everything, fearing that their little ones may miss out on an opportunity, thereby branding them as terrible parents. Dad and mom knew that I had little music ability and even less artistic ability. Athletic ability came naturally to me, so they nudged me in that direction.

In addition to reading the sports page, I loved to pour over the listings on the New York stock exchange. They encouraged reading of any kind. It fascinates me that although I had little interest in stocks for many years, my zeal for investing in stocks was suddenly rekindled in my late fifties. This coincided nicely with my accounting background and love of numbers. Parents should look for any area where their child's ability and passion overlap. Any parent who does is a blessing to their child.

The passion and ability of each of us is given by God. Giftedness is nothing to boast about or to be proud of. Even the motivation to succeed is God-given. As the apostle Paul wrote in I Corinthians 4:7, "For who makes you differ from another? And what do you have that you did not receive? Now if you did indeed receive it, why do you boast as if you had not received it?"

Putting It All Together

We are God's masterpiece. He began His marvelous work on our behalf before time began. He continued His work as He formed us in our mother's womb. Our hair and eye color, our likes and dislikes, our mental abilities, our physical talents, our social skills, and innumerable other traits were formed as our mothers carried us. In Psalm 139:14-16, David writes, "I will praise You, for I am fearfully and wonderfully made. Marvelous are Your works, and that my soul knows very well. My frame was not hidden from You, when I was made in secret, and skillfully wrought in the lowest parts of the earth. Your eyes saw my substance, being yet unformed. And in Your book they all were written. The days fashioned for me, when as yet there were none of them."

After birth, life is a gift of God. Every good thing that we experience in this life is a manifestation of His grace. As James notes in James 1:17, " Every good gift and every perfect gift is from above, and comes down from the Father of lights, with whom there is no variation or shadow of turning." He is worthy of our praise!

Chapter 2 – God's Grace in Salvation

The most important day of my life was January 21, 1978. It was the day that I settled my eternal destiny forever. Although some people who belong to Jesus don't remember a specific day or time when they surrendered their life to the Lordship of Jesus Christ, everyone is saved from their sins absolutely, unconditionally, and irrevocably at a specific point in time. A person's wedding day, birth of their first child, or graduation from high school or college are momentous occasions. Nothing, however, can compare to the day a person receives the gift of eternal life, has his sins forgiven, and becomes a child of the living God.

Grace before Time

Although there is a specific point in time when a person trusts in Jesus' death on the cross to pay for his sins, God's grace began to be poured out upon that person before the world began. Let these verses melt your heart as you reflect upon God sovereignly choosing you by His grace to belong to Him forever.

Just as <u>He chose us in Him before the foundation of the world,</u> that we should be holy and without blame before Him in love" (Ephesians 1:4).

"…who (God) has saved us and called us with a holy calling, not according to our works, <u>but according to His own purpose and grace which was given to us in Christ Jesus before time began</u>" (II Timothy 1:9).

The verse that most clearly explains which people choose to trust in Jesus as Savior and submit to Him as their Lord is Acts 13:48, "Now when the Gentiles heard this, they were glad and glorified the word of the Lord. <u>And as many as had been appointed to eternal life believed.</u>"

God's love and grace was poured out on me before time began. By faith I reached out and accepted that grace, a grace that I was destined to receive before I was ever born. That grace can be yours too if you confess your sins, trust Jesus' death on the cross to pay for the punishment of your sins, and humbly surrender to Him as your Master and Lord. If you make that choice, it will be the greatest day of your life!

Grace in the Little Things

God's fingerprints are often clearly seen as we look back upon the events of our lives. While we are in the moment, the fingerprints are hidden from our sight. As I look back I clearly see God's hand in my choice of a college to attend. My choice was Ohio University in Athens, Ohio. I chose Ohio University because my cousin Caesar graduated from Ohio University and had a favorable experience.

Ohio University also had a reputable accounting program and an outstanding baseball team. A warmer climate than Pittsburgh didn't hurt, but the real reason that I went to Ohio University was that God was moving to begin the process of drawing me to His Son Jesus. Proverbs 20:24 says, "A man's steps are of the Lord; how then can a man understand his own way?" We usually understand what God is doing when we reflect back upon our steps.

Grace in the People He Brings Our Way

I don't ever remember hearing the gospel of Jesus Christ growing up. I think that I likely never did hear the good news that Jesus died for me personally and would have died for me if I was the only person who was ever born.

That all changed my sophomore year at Ohio University. God began to surround me with people who believed that the forgiveness of sins is by faith alone in Jesus alone for the glory of God alone. The person who the Lord used the most in my life was a young lady named Suzanne. Suzanne became my best friend in college. We never dated, but we practiced softball, ate Baskin Robbins ice cream, and enjoyed mutual friends together. The most important thing that she did was tell me Bible story after Bible story. Most of the stories were new to me and the gospel was brand new. She also recruited other Christians to pray for me. People like Suzanne are described by our Lord in John 4:37-38, "For in this the saying is true: 'One sows and another reaps.' I sent you to reap that for which you have not labored; others have labored and you have entered into their labors."

Suzanne labored faithfully. For more than two years, she was a good friend and a faithful witness for Jesus. No one was happier when I finally surrendered my life to Jesus than Suzanne. I believe that there is a special reward for those who do the hard work of tilling the rocky soil of a person's heart. Any follower of Jesus can do this challenging work that eventually leads to a person expressing saving faith in Jesus.

Grace in Bringing Hardships Our Way

With Suzanne and others sharing the gospel, living imperfect but godly lives, and praying faithfully for me, you might think that giving my life to Jesus would be easy. Like so many before me, I needed God to bring disappointments and failure in to my life first. The Old Testament prophets frequently saw little or no results from their preaching ministry. God frequently softens people's hearts through trials and afflictions.

We all start our spiritual journey by building idols in our hearts. An idol is anything or anyone that we treasure more than the one true God. Ezekiel 14:3 states, "Son of man, these men have set up their idols in their hearts, and put before them that which causes them to stumble into iniquity. Should I let Myself be inquired of at all by them?"

My three biggest idols were baseball, girls, and grades, in that order. The baseball idol fell first when I failed to make the Ohio University baseball team as a freshman. Girls and grades were still occupying the number one and two spots in my heart through the first trimester of my senior year. Then nearly simultaneously, a girl that I had my eye on resisted my charming ways and I had a below average, straight B's, trimester in school. All three of my idols had failed me and the Spirit of God began closing in. Followers of Jesus should be especially aware of times when unsaved family members and friends are experiencing disappointments and hardships in their life. The Holy Spirit may be ready to usher a new soul into the kingdom of heaven.

The Day of Salvation

God had stripped me of my idols. I was feeling miserable when I woke up on January 21, 1978. Life was spinning out of control. Self-pity was consuming my thoughts and God was pursuing me. I vividly remember spending that morning cursing and swearing. The misery that I felt inside intensified. The greatest day of my life began as the worst day of my life.

Fighting God is a losing battle. He can break a person's will effortlessly. Even after a person comes to Jesus, God graciously yet firmly conquers a person's heart so that doing God's will is a delight. Jesus beautifully describes this in Matthew 11:28-30, "Come to Me, all you who labor and are heavy laden, and I will give you rest. Take My yoke upon you and learn from Me, for I am gentle and lowly in heart, and you will find rest for your souls. For My yoke is easy and My burden is light." The greatest fight (battle) of my life, getting right with God on His terms, was about to end that evening.

That afternoon I received an invitation from my friend, Karen, to go ice skating. I reasoned anything was better than staying in the apartment by myself, so I agreed. The time spent ice skating was uneventful and we decided to go back to Karen's dormitory room.

While in her room, Karen must have sensed the heaviness in my spirit. She told me that I needed to have faith like a child. I asked her what she meant and she said, "Wait, I'll go get Smitty." Smitty was a junior, a baseball player, and one of the most gifted evangelists I have ever met. He led dozens of students to Christ in his four years at Ohio University. God was bringing in the closer.

Karen found Smitty who also brought his friend Bill with him. Bill was a short Italian from Pittsburgh who had placed His trust in Jesus and His death on the cross alone a year or so earlier. Bill didn't say much, and he didn't need to talk. I understood that God had brought him to me that evening to show me that Jesus died for someone who was a lot like me. Smitty shared truth from the book of Revelation and then proceeded to share the tract, "Four Spiritual Laws," with me. I was tired physically, broken emotionally, and convinced mentally. I asked Jesus to be my Lord and Savior. It's hard to say if I was genuinely saved at that moment or fifteen minutes later when Smitty introduced me to a room full of Christians. It was then that I thought, "This is what I've been wanting" and surrendered my heart to Christ. The words of Jesus became my personal experience, "If anyone desires to come after Me, let him deny himself, and take up his cross daily, and follow Me. For whoever desires to save his life will lose it, but whoever loses his life for My sake will save it," (Luke 9:23-24). Immediately the Lord became real to me. I didn't walk to my apartment that night; it seemed like I floated back. Life would never be the same. My days on earth and eternity would be changed forever. It would determine who I would marry, the vocation that I would choose, and how I analyzed every issue of life. The Bible would become my favorite book, bringing glory to God would become my purpose, and living in God's presence would become my greatest delight. In the words of Paul, "and He dies for all, that those who live should live no longer for themselves, but for Him who died for them and rose again" (II Corinthians 5:15). In that same chapter Paul wrote, "Therefore, if anyone is in Christ, he is a new creation; old things have passed away; behold, all things have become new" (II Corinthians 5:17).

I spent a little over the first 3 ½ years in college without a personal relationship with the Lord Jesus Christ. I was a follower of the Lord only the last five months of my college experience.. I have more wonderful memories during those last 5 months than the prior 3 ½ years. There is nothing like knowing God personally. It is why we were created. Life can only be lived to the fullest when we know Him personally, have our sins forgiven, and experience His presence in our lives. In John 10:10 Jesus say, "The thief does not come except to steal, and to kill, and to destroy. I have come that they have life, and that they may have it more abundantly." On the night that the Lord was betrayed, He prayed this to God the Father. "And this is eternal life, that they may know You, the only true God, and Jesus Christ whom you have sent," (John 17:3).

The rest of my life and the rest of this book will explain how God's grace is poured out in every area of life. Coming to saving faith in Christ is the first installment of grace that a believer will enjoy for the rest of his life and throughout all eternity.

Chapter 3 – God's Grace in Marriage

So much of who we are and who we become is hard-wired into us from birth. These desires, inclinations, passions, and attractions affect future choices that we will make in our lives. Once a person gives their life to Jesus Christ, these desires become even stronger and more persuasive. As Paul writes in Philippians 2:13, "For it is God who works in you both to will and to do for His good pleasure." David wrote in Psalm 37:4, "Delight yourself also in the Lord, and He shall give you the desires of your heart." The implication is that God will put His desires in your heart as you find your daily pleasure in Him.

Even before I trusted in Jesus alone for my salvation, I had built in desires that would influence who I would marry. It all began with a desire to be married. I always had this desire even as a young boy. I was always attracted to shorter girls. They certainly had to be shorter than me! This was a social expectation when I was growing up. The long leggy type was appealing to other guys, but they were not appealing to me. Unfortunately, I also had a high opinion of myself. Yes, pride was a big weakness in most areas of my life, but when it came to choosing girlfriends or a wife, it was an asset. I figured that I deserved someone special! So I pursued young ladies who I thought were attractive, bright, and socially capable. All of these qualities were part of how God created me and this drew me to be attracted to the woman who would eventually become my wife.

God's Providence

In every other area of life, God is working through people and circumstances in the midst of the minute details and large decisions of life. It is no different when it comes to directing us to our life long companion.

God's guiding hand began when I chose to work for Coopers & Lybrand in Pittsburgh instead of Arthur Anderson in Columbus, Ohio. Both were big eight accounting firms and both had made me generous offers coming out of college. My familiarity with Pittsburgh, having family nearby, and the quality of the staff at Coopers and Lybrand informed my decision. God continued His guidance in my life when I chose to start in August of 1978, instead of June, July, or September. One of my fellow employees, who also began in August, was Becky Herbst. I began to share the gospel with Becky a few days after meeting her. She noted that I sounded a lot like her sister, Kathy, regarding what I believed. I said, "I would like to meet your sister Kathy." She gave me Kathy's phone number. I called her, and she invited me to a young adult Bible study. I went to that Bible study regularly. In God's providence, my future wife lived in the house where it was held. Her sister and brother-in-law led the study in God's Word and worship.

I was 22 ½ years old, a college graduate, and just getting settled in my new found faith. Melinda was about to turn 17, in high school, and had grown up in the ways of the Lord. All that to say, we didn't begin dating right away.

A turning point took place a little over a year later. I had begun to attend the church where Melinda grew up and heard that her mother had an operation scheduled. I had a week of vacation, so I decided that I would visit her in the hospital. I had on a pair of rather short shorts and tube socks. I also had a nice summer tan. I walked into the hospital - underdressed. Melinda's mother must have thought I was on the hunt for a wife. She asked me while in her hospital bed if I had a girlfriend. I said, "No, I don't." She promised to pray for me. Less than two years later I married her daughter! As James writes in James 5:16, "Confess your trespasses to one another, and pray for one another, that you may be healed. The effective, fervent prayer of a righteous man avails much." Mothers need to be careful how they pray for single men! They may end up marrying their daughter. The prayers of God's people make a difference and influences the lives of those we love.

The Wait

One of the most challenging aspects of the Christian life is waiting on the Lord. I have watched countless young people run out of patience, anxiously pursue someone from the opposite sex, and settle on a marriage partner who is less than God's best for them. Waiting on the Lord is never easy but always worth it, so much so that the Lord has promised to help you to wait upon Him. As David wrote in Psalm 27:14, "Wait on the Lord; be of good courage, and He shall strengthen your heart; wait, I say, on the Lord!" Jeremiah notes in Lamentations 3:25-26 "The Lord is good to those who wait for Him, to the soul who seeks Him. It is good that one should hope and wait quietly for the salvation of the Lord."

As a young person waits for God to bring the right person into his or her life and for the relationship to begin in earnest, I would humbly recommend a threefold plan. I would begin by asking God for the strength and patience to wait. Psalm 27:14 clearly states that He will strengthen our hearts. It's never beneficial to be desperate for a man or woman.

I also would encourage any young person to rest in God's will. It's the safest place for any person to be. When did the first man receive his wife? "And the Lord God caused a deep sleep to fall on Adam, and he slept; and He took one of his ribs, and closed up the flesh in its place" (Genesis 2:21). Adam literally rested when God brought his wife Eve to him. Today a person rests in God's will when He trusts God to bring his future marriage partner to him and when he focuses on doing what he already knows to be God's will. This includes developing one's personal walk with God, serving the Lord through the local church, and developing skills in a career. Resting in the Lord includes doing what we know He wants us to do at the present time.

To the ladies I would say, "Do not pursue the guy you are interested in." Every young lady wants to be picked or chosen by her special young man. Let him pick you! There are one hundred and one ways you can subtly let him know that you are interested, but let the man take the initiative. To the young man I would say, "be a man and go for it." If you are going to be the leader in your home, you need to start off on the right foot. She will respect you and you will respect yourself. Keep in mind Proverbs 18:22, "He who finds a wife finds a good thing, and obtains favor from the Lord."

<u>Know What to Look For</u>

In the business world, it is widely claimed that roughly 1 in 3 hires are successful. In light of how much time, money, and analysis goes into the process that is an astounding reality. I would say that any good fit for a job requires two things. The employer must know the qualities a person needs to do the job, and there must be a large amount of God's grace guiding the process. I believe the same can be said about finding a marriage partner that is the right fit.

The Bible is quite clear on the kind of lady who will be an exemplary wife. I refer to her as "The Humble Helper." Humble is her defining character quality and helper defines her conduct or the focus of her life. In I Peter 3:5-6 we read, "For in this manner, in former times, the holy women who trusted in God also adorned themselves, being submissive to their own husbands, as Sarah obeyed Abraham, calling him lord, whose daughters you are if you do good and are not afraid with any terror." In this passage, Sarah's humility is expounded in a number of ways. She obeyed Abraham when he timidly told her to say that she was his sister and not his wife. This temporarily caused her to be part of Abimelech's harem. She also humbly trusted God, and God protected Sarah before she was morally compromised. She humbly went along with Abraham's plan. She respected him demonstrated by her calling him "lord." All men need to be honored and respected. It's how God makes men. Sarah demonstrated humility by trusting God, obeying Abraham, and by calling Abraham lord. A humble wife is a gift from God.

Her life is to be consumed by the strong desire to serve others, especially her husband. When Adam realized that he too needed a companion, "And the Lord God said, 'It is not good that man should be alone; I will make him a helper comparable to him'" (Genesis 2:18). Most men desperately need help! That is why God created women. A young man should look for a young lady who fits the job description, "Humble Helper."

There is no shortage of Biblical material about the job description of a husband. The most complete picture of what a young lady should look for in a man is found in Ephesians 5:25-29. "Husbands, love your wives, just as Christ also loved the church and gave Himself for her, that He might sanctify and cleanse her with the washing of water by the word, that He might present her to Himself a glorious church, not having spot or wrinkle or any such thing, but that she should be holy and without blemish. So husbands ought to love their own wives as their own bodies; he who loves his wife loves himself. For no one ever hated his own flesh, but nourishes and cherishes it, just as the Lord does the church."

The job description of an excellent husband can also be summarized in two words, "Loving Leader." How should a husband exhibit love towards his wife? Paul specifies three ways. He must be committed to loving his wife (5:25). This means that he must be willing to make sacrifices for her. This includes when she is unlovely. Jesus sacrificed for us when we were unlovely, likewise a husband should make sacrifices when his wife is moody, bossy, or emotional. He must also be concerned about her purity (5:26-27). Jesus died for us so that the word of God would save us and sanctify us, or make us holy. Making sure that our wives are in God's Word and in church are prime ways that we can show concern for their purity. Wives need their spiritual tanks filled. Lastly, a husband must care for her needs (5:28-29). He must care for her physical needs by providing for her. That is the meaning of the word "nourish." A husband should also care for her emotional needs by "cherishing" her. Blessed is the woman who finds a man who can meet this high standard.

It is the grace of God that brings a Humble Helper into the life of a man. It is the grace of God that brings a Loving Leader into the life of a woman. Even if we know what we are looking for, it takes the wisdom and grace of God to help us evaluate a person properly. So many things can go wrong when we are evaluating someone who has potential to be our marriage partner. People tend to put their best foot forward when they are trying to impress someone. We can be easily deceived. People also change after they are married. Circumstances change dramatically after a couple starts a family and the dynamics between a husband and wife can change drastically too. Only God can see the future. We can minimize our risk by knowing what makes a good husband or wife, but we need His grace to pick the right spouse and to be the right spouse.

The 20% Principle

My wife, Melinda, was blessed to have a godly mentor, Mrs. Teague. Mrs. Teague was the pastor's wife of the church Melinda attended from ten years old until she was twenty. One of the sayings that Mrs. Teague left with Melinda was that in a good marriage a wife will love 80% of her husband's qualities. The other 20% she can learn to live with as part of the marriage agreement. I'm sure that there are qualities of mine that Melinda wishes were different. In fact, I could easily name a few. Melinda is a treasure to me, but has yet to reach sinless perfection. What do we do with the 20% of the other person that we do not like?

We know that constant complaining to the other person is not the answer. In Proverbs 19:13 we read "A foolish son is the ruin of his father, and the contentions of a wife are a continual dripping." Few things in life can drive a person crazy more than an otherwise quiet room punctuated by a dripping faucet. Although wives seem to be more prone to this annoying habit, they don't have a monopoly on it!

We also know that bullying, inducing guilt trips, and frequently lecturing one's spouse will make matters worse. If these ill-fated methods don't work, what is a husband or wife to do with the undesirable 20%?

A good place to begin is by thanking God for your spouse and the 80% that you do love. God gave your spouse and that 80% to you as a gift. Focusing on the qualities that you love is a great place to start. It will help you live with the 20% that you don't like.

Ask God through prayer to help change your attitude about the character qualities and habits in your spouse that you don't like. Being content or satisfied in any area of life is a wonderful gift from God. It can transform any darkness in our life and make it light. In I Timothy 6:6 we read, "Now godliness with contentment is great gain."

Ask God to show you if your behavior is making your spouse's weakness even more annoying. I remember early in our marriage when I was frustrated with Melinda for feeling overwhelmed. After all, she was merely a wife of a seminarian, a mother of a two year old who was a handful, a young lady adjusting to being away from home, and a wife who saw little of a husband who was hustling while being a full-time student and part-time accountant! I didn't realize that part of her feeling overwhelmed was that I was expecting near perfection from her in every area of life. God revealed my glaring weakness to me in a Sunday school class. I confessed my sin and tried to be part of the solution, not part of the problem.

When all else fails, pray for your spouse. God is the author of all meaningful change from the inside out. It certainly beats complaining, bullying, inducing guilt trips, and frequently lecturing him or her. "The king's heart (and your spouse's heart) is in the hand of the Lord, like the rivers of water; He turns it wherever He wishes" (Proverbs 21:1).

The Grace of Life

A healthy marriage is a gift from God; to love and be loved is the yearning of the human heart. Peter refers to husbands and wives, "as being heirs together of the grace of life." Marriage can be a wonderful experience or it can be an exceedingly painful experience. There is only so much one person can do to make a marriage healthy, life-giving, and a joy. It takes the grace of God to find the right person, be the right person, and live together as one person. May God give each of us the measure of grace needed for a marriage that is Christ- honoring.

Chapter 4 – God's Grace in Raising a Family

Wanting A Family

God's word is clear when it comes to whether a married couple should want to have a family. In Psalm 127:3-5 we read, "Behold, children are a heritage from the Lord, the fruit of the womb is a reward. Like arrows in the hand of a warrior, so are the children of one's youth. Happy is the man who has his quiver full of them; they shall not be ashamed, but shall speak with their enemies in the gate." A few salient thoughts from this text are in order. Children are a blessing from God, starting young is a good idea, and children are an asset (enemies will think twice before attacking you) and not a liability. All these truths from these verses are under attack today.

In Genesis 33, Jacob is about to meet his estranged brother, Esau, after a separation of roughly twenty years. In verses 4 & 5 we read, "But Esau ran to meet him, and embraced him, and fell on his neck and kissed him, and they wept. And he lifted his eyes and saw the women and children, and said, "Who are these with you?" so he said, "The children whom God has graciously given your servant.""

Jacob had a divine perspective when it came to his children. At this point he had eleven sons and one daughter, and he saw each one of them as a gift from God, given to Him by God's grace.

This perspective has diminished in the American culture. Children are oftentimes not seen to be a gift given by God as an expression of His grace. The primary reasons given for not wanting children are that they are too expensive, they reduce a couple's freedom, and this world is too evil to have children. Young couples look at me as if to say, "Pastor Joe, when you were young, it was easier to make ends meet. Financial burdens were lighter. The world wasn't as bad. You just don't understand."

Allow me to tell my story and you be the judge if these assertions have merit. Melinda and I had been married for approximately one and a half years when we had two decisions to make. Should I stay in accounting or go to seminary to train for pastoral ministry? After graduating from college in clinical dietetics, should Melinda get a job as a dietician or should we try to start a family? We followed the Lord's strong leading. I left accounting, went to seminary, and Melinda immediately conceived and our firstborn, Dan, was born.

While in Grace Seminary, I earned $5.00 an hour for my first year in school and $8.65 an hour my last two years. Both figures were small percentages of what I earned as a CPA. Every month we drew down from our considerable savings. So what did we do after two years in seminary? We tried to expand our family and God blessed us with our second child, our only daughter, Marianne.

My first ministry assignment was church planting in a suburb of Cleveland, Ohio. We had a regular salary, but our savings had pretty much evaporated. So what did we do? We asked God to graciously give us another child which He did. Our third child, Tony, was born.

We moved to southcentral Pennsylvania where I pastored an established church, Palmyra Grace Brethren Church. A few years later, Melinda suffered a miscarriage. Money was fairly tight with three children, a mortgage, and a stay at home mother. We decided to trust God one more time, and he granted us our wish of blessing us with our third son and fourth child, Joe Jr.

When is a good time to have children? If my story communicates anything, it is this. It's never a good time to have children financially nor will children ever expand your freedom. It is always a good time to have children when it comes to fulfillment and fun. All four of our adult kids are wonderful. Our lives are enriched by each one of them.

Having and raising children is an adventure in faith. "For we walk by faith, not by sight" (II Corinthians 5:7). Having children is part of that faith walk. Raising four kids wasn't always easy, but it has been one of the great disbursements of God's grace in my life.

Raising Your Kids Requires God's Grace

By now you probably have guessed that I am going to conclude that the most important ingredient to successfully raising kids is the outpouring of God's grace in their lives. God certainly uses good parenting, but good parenting is less of a factor than God doing what only He can do in the life of your child. That truth explains why good parents can raise a bad child and bad parents can raise a child who turns out great. There is no sure fire program to follow that produces wonderful children.

That being said, the fundamentals of sound parenting are a tool that God uses to produce children who grow to be quality young men and women. What are the fundamentals of sound parenting?

Love Your Kids

The first, and universally embraced, fundamental is to love your children. Any good parent has his or her child's best interest at heart. Sacrifice, compassion, tenderness, encouragement, and seeing the potential in the child are all features of loving your child. Mothers have a natural bent when it comes to loving their own children. We might say they champion the cause of loving their children. In I Thessalonians 2:7 Paul writes, "But we were gentle among you, just as a nursing mother cherishes her own children." This gentle hand of a loving mother is balanced by the firm hand of a father. In I Thessalonians 2:11 Paul writes, "As you know how we exhorted, and comforted, and charged every one of you, as a father does his own children." According to Paul a father's love propels a child forward in his development as a person. The love of a mother and father provides a powerful one-two punch that gives a child confidence and a healthy self-concept.

Discipline Your Kids

The second and far less universally embraced fundamental in raising children is to discipline your children. Let's begin with two self-evident truths. Children are precious and bring us great joy. Children are also wayward, self-willed, and in desperate need of correction. A child left to his own devices is a frightening sight.

Discipline is an expression of love. Our heavenly Father disciplines us because He loves us. In Hebrews 12:6 we read, "For whom the Lord loves He chastens, and scourges every son whom He receives." So too parents discipline their children because they love them.

God's Word and personal experience clearly proclaim that the proper method of discipline is both verbal, and if not obeyed, physical. When children don't obey, they may need some assistance. The rod applied to the rump followed by an affectionate hug is the proper means of discipline. Contemporary methods such as "time out" and "time in" appeal to our "soft culture," but do not supplant the wisdom of Almighty God. What are some reasons that God's old-fashioned mode of discipline is to be preferred over modern day substitutes?

Nothing corrects a child like the rod. In Proverbs 22:15, "Foolishness is bound up in the heart of a child; the rod of correction will drive it far from him." The word "bound up" means tightly bound or tied. Foolishness comes naturally to children. Nothing knocks the foolishness out like the rod.

When I was about eight years old, my parents built an addition to our little home in Pennsylvania. As a result there was a large dirt pile in our backyard. Our driveway was narrow, steep, and great for riding bicycles and skateboards. You could pick up pretty good speed going down that driveway. The dirt pile was in the grass at the bottom of the driveway. One evening my brother, Marc, was riding a skateboard down the driveway. I stood next to the dirt pile and began throwing "dirt bombs" in the air as my brother came full speed down the driveway. My goal was to hit him on the head as he came down the driveway. It took timing, accuracy, and the right arc to hit him on the head. After several near misses, I threw a dirt bomb that had great potential. As it was coming down, I called to my brother, "Marc, look up." He did, and the dirt bomb hit him in the eye. He screamed, ran in the house, and explained what happened. My father gave me the number one spanking of my life. He rushed Marc to the emergency room. When he came home, he explained that Marc almost lost sight in his eye and proceeded to give me the second worst spanking of my life. Although I was less than the perfect child, after that, I never did anything that foolish again. The rod drove the foolishness far from me.

Another reason to utilize God's manner of discipline is that you will enjoy your children. In Proverbs 29:15 and 17 we read, "The rod and rebuke give wisdom, but a child left to himself brings shame to his mother. Correct your son, and he will give you rest; yes, he will give delight to your soul." Both physical, the rod, and verbal, rebuke, combined gives your child wisdom. In other words, you can wear yourself out explaining to your child what is right and what is wrong. Their actions would seem to indicate that they don't understand. So the parent explains the same thing over and over again. One properly administered discipline and suddenly their IQ jumps 30 points! They are wise. They get it! It is then that they bring delight and pleasure to the hearts of their parents.

Proper discipline trains the child to submit to the Lord. Loving discipline, not applied in anger, trains a child to be obedient to the Lord. There is nothing more fulfilling for a parent than to have a child that grows up wanting to obey and please the Lord. As John wrote in 3 John 4, "I have no greater joy than to hear that my children walk in truth." John is referring to spiritual children. It applies equally to biological children as well.

It's important to note that most children do not need a lot of physical discipline. After a few "events," the mere possibility of another "event" is sufficient to motivate most children to obey. In our home in Pennsylvania, we placed a thin dial rod above the frame of every door in every room. It made discipline quite handy. We rarely had to use the dial rods. Usually we merely had to look up at one and a correction in behavior or attitude was instantaneous! God uses properly executed discipline to graciously mold the hearts of children.

Be a Good Example to Your Kids

Isn't it wonderful that being a good example is the goal and not being a perfect example? More is caught than taught. This is true of boys and men in particular. Some of the things that we pass on by example are important and significant such as our priorities, convictions, and how we love God and people. Others are less significant such as clearing our throat before we speak, smiling when we are nervous, or slapping people on the back as a way of affirming them.

Some habits that we pass on are positive and others are negative. I use to have the bad habit of opening the refrigerator door and drinking milk or orange juice straight from the carton. That is until the day that our four year old son, Dan, was standing right beside me carefully watching each gulp. That was the last time I drank directly from anything in the refrigerator. That was certainly not a habit that I wanted to see passed on to my child!

The apostle Paul was keenly aware of the power of imitation. In I Corinthians 11:1 we read, "Imitate me, just as I also imitate Christ." The word "imitate" is the Greek word from which we get the English word "mimic." Children mimic us more than we think. In Philippians 4:9 Paul writes, "The things which you learned and received and heard and saw in me, these do, and the God of peace will be with you." Imitating includes learning, hearing, and seeing the life of others.

Our kids tend to imitate our way of handling money, whether we trust God with trials in our lives, whether we love church more than sports, and in a multitude of other ways. How they respond to money and possessions is especially caught more than taught. Our four kids fondly remember going to the Turkey Hill convenient store after church on Sunday mornings. I would usually buy them each their favorite flavor slush. I didn't buy them one every Sunday, because I wanted them to be grateful for the treat and not to take it for granted. I chose to not buy them a slush about once a month. Our youngest child, Joe Jr., was in the four to eight year old range and he figured out my pattern. He knew that if it had been about a month since they had not received a slush treat, he would mentally prepare for the disappointment and was either pleasantly surprised when I brought one out or was fine with not getting one if I didn't. Through this and other means, our kids learned to be content with what they had and to be grateful when they received something unexpectedly.

Another important way that we influence our kids is by consistent repetition of the things that we do and say. One of the things that I said countless times to our kids when growing up was, "You say Joe, how can we know God's will?" The question is from a John MacArthur sermon on discerning God's will in our lives. Of course John said, "You say, John, how can we know God's will?" I asked this question so many times when we had decisions to make that our kids ask themselves the same question as they live life as adults. It's amazing how much of life is caught rather than taught.

Teach Your Kids

The compliment to being a good example to our kids is to teach them the ways of the Lord. When our teaching and our living line up, we give the Holy Spirit more to work with in forming virtues in our children. A good Bible-believing church can reinforce the solid teaching of parents, but the primary responsibility lies in the home.

In Deuteronomy 6:6-9 we read, "And these words which I command you today shall be in your heart. You shall teach them diligently to your children, and shall talk of them when you sit in your house, when you walk by the way, when you lie down, and when you rise up. You shall bind them as a sign on your hand, and they shall be as frontlets between your eyes. You shall write them on the doorposts of your house and on your gates." This wonderful passage instructs parents to have God's Word in their hearts, that is, to have it on the forefront of their minds and thoughts. Then when teaching moments present themselves, talk about His word anytime and anyplace. Show your kids that you love God's Word.

Ideally start teaching your kids when they are young. Sometimes parents come to Jesus when the kids are a little older. Better late than never is the truism for that situation. Timothy was blessed to have an early start in learning God's Word. Paul notes in II Timothy 3:15, "and that from childhood you have known the Holy Scriptures, which are able to make you wise for salvation through faith which is in Christ Jesus." Young minds are impressionable. Imprint the gospel in their moldable minds, the sooner the better.

One tradition that Melinda and I practiced was what we called, "Bible time." Most evenings while our kids were growing up, we would sit around the living room and read our Bibles together. If we missed a night or two because of schedules, we were not hard on ourselves. Perfection is impossible. Consistency is attainable. When a child was old enough to read, he took a turn reading a verse during Bible time. I would periodically ask a pertinent question. Kids love to read out loud and to be asked their opinion which they readily offer. We had plenty of laughs and actually encouraged laughter during our time in God's Word. If nothing else, Bible time impressed upon our kids that mom and dad loved God's Word and that we wanted them to love it too. I encourage fathers to initiate a time of Bible reading and discussions with their family.

Pray for Your Kids

You might be thinking, "This is great. If I just love my children, discipline my children, be a good example for my children, and teach my children God's Word, then they will love God and His Word. That is, they will turn out great! They will be all that God wants them to be. After all Proverbs 22:6 says, "Train up a child in the way he should go, and when he is old he will not depart from it." It's true, that is what Proverbs 22:6 says. The book of Proverbs is a collection of true, God-breathed proverbial sayings. They are not a collection of promises. They are wise sayings that a wise person should live by and if a person does He will experience the blessings of God. That is why the final fundamental of good parenting is to pray regularly and fervently for your children.

Prayer moves the Hand that moves the world and that includes the hearts of your kids. God can work on your kid's heart and when He does it is an act of grace. We don't earn or deserve His grace when He works inside our kids. They ultimately become what they become by the grace of God. In Hebrews 13:20a and 13:21 we read, "Now may the God of peace…make you complete in every good work to do His will, working in you what is well pleasing in His sight, through Jesus Christ, to whom be glory forever and ever. Amen." The Lord is the one who works in us what is well pleasing in His sight. This includes the lives of our kids.

It has been said that Christian parents put too much blame on themselves when their kids veer off the Jesus track and take too much credit when they stay on the Jesus track. I believe that this statement is true. God is the One who saves our kids, gives them the desire to follow Him wholeheartedly, gives them a heart for His word, helps them overcome trials and temptations, steers them towards good friendships, produces the fruit of the Spirit in their lives, and dozens of other virtuous qualities. That is why the most important fundamental of parenting is to pray regularly and fervently for your kids. More than anything else it triggers the grace of God to work in them.

As They Get Older

As our kids grow and age, the dynamic between them and their parents ideally changes. The early formative years could be called, "the era of the law." Boundaries are set, obedience is learned, and the parent endeavors to build godly habits in the child's life. The era of the law lasts roughly until the age of twelve.

Then the young person enters into the era of grace. Parents should start to move the young person towards independence. Little by little, the freedom to choose is granted. Failure is accepted as a normal part of maturity and growth. More freedom is granted as good choices are made.

The final goal is to have a wise son or daughter, one who lives life skillfully as an independent adult. One who lives life skillfully is synonymous with being wise. The source of all wisdom is God. In Proverbs 2:6 we read, "For the Lord gives wisdom; from His mouth come knowledge and understanding." Nothing brings a parent more joy than to have a grown adult offspring living life wisely. "A wise son makes a glad father" (Proverbs 10:1a). We as parents should thank God for wise, adult children. He is the one who imparts wisdom in their hearts. This is one of the greatest manifestations of His divine grace.

One of the joys in my life is to see my adult kids demonstrate greater wisdom in their lives than I did when I was their age. They are ultimately His children and He is more committed to them living life with excellence than my wife or I. When it is all said and done, we can do our best and pray that our best is blessed by God.

Chapter 5 – God's Grace in Fulfilling Your Calling

We spend a great deal of time at work over the course of our lifetime. Approximately two thousand hours a year is invested in a full-time job. It stands to reason that God wants to utilize our vocational calling to provide for our daily needs and to honor Him. In Ephesians 2:10 we read, "For we are His workmanship, created in Christ Jesus for good works, which God prepared beforehand that we should walk in them." We are most effective and fulfilled when we are doing the pre-planned good works that God pre-ordained for us to do. This includes the good work done while working.

<u>Grace in Finding What to He Wants Us to Do</u>

I spent seven years working as a Certified Public Accountant. I earned a good living. I had a respected position. I also was miserable. During my pre-seminary days, I discovered five principles from Jeremiah 1 that God used to show me that I was called by Him to be a pastor. Four of these principles provide guidance to any vocational calling that God may be directing you towards. One, I believe, is unique to the call into full-time Christian service.

The first timeless principle is that our vocational calling is **initiated by God.** "Then the word of the Lord came to me saying: "Before I formed you in the womb; I knew you; before you were born I sanctified you; I ordained you a prophet to the nations" (Jeremiah 1:4-5). Here we see that God initiated Jeremiah's call to be a prophet. God intimately knew Jeremiah before he was conceived and formed in his mother's womb. God set Jeremiah apart for his prophetic ministry and ordained or divinely appointed him for this task. Jeremiah did not campaign to be a prophet. He did not direct his course of study to be a prophet. God initiated the call to a prophetic ministry and began to prepare Him for his vocational calling before he was conceived. God's Hand is on our lives, before our parents aspired to have us.

The second timeless principle is that we feel **inadequate to do the job.** "Then said I: 'Ah, Lord God! Behold, I cannot speak, for I am a youth," (Jeremiah 1:6). Every job and vocation has its challenges. We should feel a little bit over our heads. God wants this. He wants us to be dependent upon Him. He wants us to trust Him. He desires us to give Him praise and glory for our successes. If the Lord is involved in our vocational choice, it will be accompanied by a feeling of inadequacy to do the job apart from Him.

A third timeless principle is that we are **indebted to respond.** "But the Lord said to me: "Do not say, 'I am a youth,' for you shall go to all to whom I send you, and whatever I command you, you shall speak" (Jeremiah 1:7). God did not allow Jeremiah's excuse that he was too young to gain any traction in Jeremiah's thinking. "Don't say that you are too young." Your age is irrelevant. You will speak to whom I send you and you will say what I command you to say, after all I am Almighty God. Moses had a similar dialogue with God when he tried to avoid his calling, in Exodus 3:11, 4:1, 4:10. He used every excuse he could think of, but in the end he had no choice but to respond to God. In I Corinthians 9:16, Paul writes, "For if I preach the gospel, I have nothing to boast of, <u>for necessity is laid upon</u> <u>me</u>; yes, woe is me if I do not preach the gospel!"

If your vocational calling is not full-time ministry, He may make you dissatisfied, unsuccessful, or tired of your present position. I think that it is highly unlikely that He will prepare you to spend 3 days in the belly of a large fish like Jonah! It's also unlikely that you will experience the degree of internal misery that I suffered while I wrestled with God as He was calling me into pastoral ministry. This is the one principle that does not fully apply to all vocational callings.

The fourth principle applies to us all. God gets **involved in our calling.** "Do not be afraid of their faces, for I am with you to deliver you," says the Lord. Then the Lord put forth His hand and touched my mouth, and the Lord said to me: "Behold, I have put My words in your mouth" (Jeremiah 1:8-9). God encouraged Jeremiah by giving him two promises. He promised Jeremiah that He would be present with him to protect him. Some people would respond with hostility, but God would be with Jeremiah to deliver him from their hands. If God calls us to do something, why wouldn't He be with us? "Lo, I am with you always, even to the end of the age." Matthew 28:20 is true of fulfilling the great commission. It's also a promise for every area of our lives.

God also got involved by putting His words in Jeremiah's mouth. He told Jeremiah exactly what to say. The modern equivalent to this is that God gives us the resources to succeed. Gifts and talents, the necessary background, and quality people who invest in us to help us succeed is how God gets involved today.

When I graduated from seminary I was green, very green. I was led by the Lord to plant a church in the greater Cleveland area and had no idea how badly I was in over my head. We had no people, except our family of four, to start the church. God surrounded me with wonderful pastors in our district of churches. Bob Combs, Bob Fetterhoff, Bud Olszewski, and Ron Boehm were a few of the godly men who assisted me to achieve the modest level of success that we enjoyed. They were gifts of God's grace.

The final principle to discern God's direction vocationally is that God promises us **influence for Him**. "See, I have this day set you over the nations and over the kingdoms, to root out and to pull down, to destroy and to throw down, to build and to plant" (Jeremiah 1:10). Jeremiah's call was exceedingly difficult, but God promised him that he would have great influence. An entire nations' destiny would be determined by whether they heeded the words he spoke in behalf of God.

I know that the greatest influence that I could have for the Lord is to be a pastor. I could have successfully done a few other things, but my greatest impact is accomplished by doing what He created and called me to do. The same is true for you. Be patient, give God time, and He will direct you to the vocation and specific place that will maximize your influence for Him.

Grace When Receiving Guidance from Others

God uses other people to guide us vocationally. Other people can know things that we don't know, see things in us that we don't see, and be familiar with opportunities that are before us that we can't see.

Our daughter Marianne was struggling at work. It was an ongoing daily battle. One day her brother, Tony, came home from work, saw the downcast look on her face and said, "Why don't you apply to Smuckers. I hear that they treat their employees well." Having nothing to lose she did, secured a position with Smuckers, and has successfully worked there for seven years to date. She also met her future husband, Mike, at Smuckers too!

God uses people to help us choose a career path. He uses others to help us change our career path. He also frequently uses others to assist us in finding a better position in our present career path. These choices can be of immeasurable benefit to us, our families, and those around us as we seek to honor the Lord in our careers.

Grace to Enjoy What I Do

Work can be hard. Work is under the curse. Yet God wants us to enjoy our work. What a conundrum! I spent many days not looking forward to going to work as an accountant and a few others as a pastor. I know what it is like to grind through a week of work. I also know that I am not unique. I have listened and counseled countless people who have suffered the same plight.

On the other hand when someone enjoys their work, the week flies by, the months evaporate, and retirement comes too soon. In Ecclesiastes, Solomon captures this dilemma beautifully. "Nothing is better for a man than that he should eat and drink, and that his soul should enjoy good in his labor," Ecclesiastes 2:24. Again in chapter 3:13 he writes, "Also that every man should eat and drink and enjoy the good of all his labor—it is the gift of God." This is the same author who wrote, "Vanity of vanities, all is vanity." How can we enjoy our calling when so often it seems to be so empty, purposeless, and even the cause of pain?

I believe that there are some things that only we can do and some that only God can do. We can see every job as a gift from God. As Solomon said work is a source of material provision. It keeps us out of trouble. It gives us a sense of worth. Even a job that is drudgery is a gift from God. We also can be content. Contentment is the heart of a great deal of successful living. In 21st century America, we are better off than 99% of all people in world history. We can be satisfied today knowing that the unpleasant work situation is only temporary. In every unpleasant work situation that I have been in, God has always provided "a way of escape" (see I Corinthians 10:13) in His time. We also can be looking for another position or begin our own side business. This gives us hope that our situation will improve soon. Hope is like oxygen. We desperately need it, especially when we are being mistreated by our supervisor, many of whom are in a position to make life miserable for us.

Ultimately though, we are dependent upon the grace of God for a fulfilling vocational experience. God is the One who opens doors and closes doors. He is the One who moves troublesome fellow employees on or softens the heart of unreasonable supervisors. He is the One who matches our gifts, talents, experiences, and desires with the needs and personalities of a specific place of employment. We can take numerous tests which tell us about ourselves and the potential vocations that will thrill our soul, receive great coaching from an employment agency, and ask trusted friends their opinion about where they see us fulfilled in the workplace. Only God can open doors, prepare hearts, and grant us the fulfillment that we all desire in our work. Work hard to enjoy your work. Pray harder for God's grace to make that possible.

Grace to Keep On Keeping On

It's so much easier to start a new job than to finish well in an old one. When we start a new job, we dream of a long, successful, and happy tenure. We dream of the perfect fit. We hold onto the hope that our work days will be filled with satisfaction and joy.

Then reality strikes in one form or another. My second accounting job held such promise. The company was growing and created a new position, a supervisory position, which reviewed the work of the staff accountants. They hired me for that position. I quickly found out that the firm had a revolving door. New accountants were hired and old ones left at a rapid rate. The reason was simple. The founder and managing partner was an exceedingly difficult man to work under. The culture was tense, and the work environment far less than enjoyable.

The quality that made the job intolerable for me was the conflict in values that I had with the firm. I vividly recall when the managing partner wanted me to doctor a client's records by $200,000 thereby cheating the government out of almost $100,000. I told him that I couldn't do that. He said, "You have to do it." The message was clear. He took me off the client, gave the work to a more willing employee, and my fate was sealed. Eight months later, I was let go from my position, two weeks before I was going to resign to attend seminary. I received far more money for being fired than I would have if I resigned. That's God's grace!

All of that to say, it was a daily battle to continue to work in such an unpleasant environment. When life is difficult, whether it is an arduous relationship or a painful work environment, we need God's sustaining grace. Grace that enables us to continue with dignity and respect. In II Timothy 2:1 Paul writes, "You therefore, my son, be strong in the grace that is in Christ Jesus." Timothy needed to be strengthened by God's grace and so do we.

When we are in an unmanageable position at work, it is encouraging to remember that this is a temporary hardship and that God will deliver us to enjoy a better opportunity in His time. Both of these uplifting truths are seen in I Corinthians 10:13, "No temptation has overtaken you except such as is common to man; but God is faithful, who will not allow you to be tempted beyond what you are able, but with the temptation will also make the way of escape, that you may be able to bear it." God knows exactly when and how to move us on to the next position. He knows how much we can bear, usually more than we think. Until then, it takes the Lord's sustaining grace to do our job with excellence and dignity.

Grace to Bear Fruit While Working

Our calling demands an enormous amount of our time, energy, and mental focus. If we do the simple math, we can estimate that we will work 40 hours per week times 50 weeks a year or 2,000 hours per year. If we work 40 years, we will spend an estimated 80,000 hours working during our lifetime.

It stands to reason that God wants to use us in the workplace to accomplish more than to merely earn a living. He also wants us to be a blessing to society. In fact, God wants His people to bear fruit as we work. In John 15:16 our Lord states to His apostles, "You did not choose Me, but I chose you and appointed you that you should go and bear fruit, and that your fruit should remain." Fruit bearing is the Lord's will for His apostles and for anyone who belongs to Him.

Bearing fruit can be accomplished in many ways, some of which are quite simple. Fruit bearing is the Spirit of God working in us and through us. Fruit in our lives points people to Him as we live for Him. In Hebrews 13:15 we read, "Therefore by Him let us continually offer the sacrifice of praise to God, that is, the fruit of our lips, giving thanks to His name." Praising God, especially when work is hard, is a wonderful way to show others that God is at work in us. It is an example of genuine spiritual fruit. Sharing the gospel, working without grumbling, sharing uplifting words, and serving others so that they can succeed at their work are all examples of fruit bearing.

All genuine fruit is a product of God's wonderful grace. The Holy Spirit works in us so that we operate on a supernatural plane. We do things, say things, and have godly attitudes that only He can produce in us. Take a moment to thank God for your place of employment and ask Him "to work in you what is well-pleasing in His sight" (Hebrews 13:21) and by doing so bear fruit that remains.

Chapter 6 – God's Grace in the Midst of Trials

If there is one time that everyone agrees that we are in need of God's grace, it is when we are going through trials. We feel the need for divine assistance more acutely. We may need His strength, guidance, wisdom, patience, perspective, love, or peace. Whatever the need, the pressures of trials magnifies our dependence upon God and need for His grace.

God's word uses a number of interesting words to describe the trials of life. Let's briefly look at three. In James 1:2 we read, "My brethren, count it all joy when you fall into various trials." The word "various" conveys the idea of "diverse" or "multi-varied." Trials come in a multitude of different sizes, shapes, and colors. Even similar trials have a unique twist. It's as though our loving heavenly Father tailors the trials to meet our specific spiritual needs.

On the other hand, trials are common. In I Corinthians 10:13a Paul writes, "No temptation has overtaken you except what is common to man." Each trial may be tailor made for our spiritual development, yet they share common characteristics with trials that others have experienced. Challenges to care for our increasingly dependent parent may have some unique aspects, but in other ways our challenge is quite like others in an analogous situation.

In Job 5:7 the author of Job writes, "Yet man is born to trouble, as the sparks fly upward." In other words, troubles in life are <u>not unusual</u>. Handling the difficulties of life by God's grace is an invaluable life skill. If we respond to trials well, God will use the trials to make us better. If not, we may become bitter. How a person responds to trials can make the difference between a life well lived and one that is full of sorrow and regret. Here are a few lessons that I have learned about handling trials.

<u>Lessons on How to Face Our Trials</u>

<u>Lesson #1 – Sometimes when it rains, it pours</u>

Thankfully, this is not our normal state! There are, however, seasons of life when one burden piles on top of another. When I was a young man in my mid-thirties, my Aunt Gloria passed away losing her battle with cancer, our pet cat was grazed and killed by a speeding car on our street, and we learned that our church planting effort in Eastlake, Ohio was going to close. We suffered the death of my dear Aunt, the death of our cat, and the death of our beloved church over a period of a few days. God's grace is sufficient for times like these. They don't last forever. The sun will shine and we will enjoy brighter days.

<u>Lesson #2 – God is always good</u>

No matter what happens in our life, God is always good. He is a good Heavenly Father who always and only has our best interest at heart. No matter how unexpected or painful the trial is, God remains the source of everything that is good. In Psalm 27:12-14, David wrote, "Do not deliver me to the will of my adversaries; for false witnesses have risen against me, and such as breathe out violence. <u>I would have lost heart, unless I had</u> believed that I would see the goodness of the Lord in the land of the living. Wait on the Lord; be of good courage, and He shall strengthen your heart; wait, I say, on the Lord!" Slanderous enemies were pursuing David, trying to destroy him and his reputation. David said that he would not have survived if he did not believe that he would see God's good hand in his life in the future. The goodness of God is a truth that we must intensely cling to no matter how bleak our future appears to be. It's helpful to remember that God is always crazy about me. Nothing that I do and nothing that happens to me can change that reality.

<u>Lesson #3 – God's Sovereignty is never to be doubted</u>

Life really spins out of control if we doubt that God is entirely in control. There is nothing quite like being reminded that we are not in control of our lives or the lives of others. It actually is a healthy dynamic. The difficulty comes when we don't believe that God is in control either. If that is true, we are at the mercy of blind fate, the merciless hands of others, or the worst scenario of all, the will of the evil one. God's sovereignty is a truth to rest in, not a bondage to escape. When merged with God's goodness, the peace of God will reign in the child of God as we rest in the character of God.

When we were church planting in the Cleveland area, we had a rough summer. The total number of people who called Lake County

Grace Brethren Church their home church was around fifty-five people. At the end of that summer, the number was approximately twenty-seven. It was hard, but we pressed on. A year later, we had grown to a little over forty people when we got hit with losses again. A husband had just finished his medical residency and received an offer in Lancaster, Pennsylvania. He accepted the offer. A month later, he received another offer in the Cleveland area which would have kept him, his wife, and daughter in the area and at the church plant. It was too late. The offer had been accepted to move to Pennsylvania. An officer in the Air Force had served his three years in Lake County. Air Force regulations compelled him to move. If he had one more year of accumulated service to his credit, he could have chosen to stay in the area, which he, his wife, and 3 children would have loved. They too moved, and the handwriting was on the wall for our little church.

These two situations convinced me that it was God's will for the church to close and for us to move on to our next assignment. Although sad, it opened the doors to a wonderful eleven and a half year ministry at Palmyra Grace Brethren Church. As Job so poignantly said, "Though He slay me, yet will I trust Him" (Job 13:15a). There is no better place to be than in the center of God's "good, acceptable, and perfect will" (Romans 12:2b).

Lesson #4 – It pays to trust God immediately with our trials

The Lord impressed this lesson upon me over a three year period. He first brought this lesson to my attention on the night of our daughter, Marianne, and son-in-law, Michael's rehearsal dinner.

We came home after 9:00 p.m. that Friday night only to find that our house was flooded. An overflowing bathroom sink on the upper floor caused the water to flow down to the main floor and eventually down to the basement floor. It wasn't pretty! As one who was co-officiating my daughter's wedding the next day, I was forced to pray immediately to God, trusting Him that everything would be fine. The wedding was beautiful, and the flood triggered much needed home repairs and remodeling.

About a year later, our daughter-in-law, Kim, was having a difficult pregnancy that had resulted in a few trips to the hospital. One Sunday afternoon, our son Dan called to tell us that Kim was in the hospital again. We were asked to pray that her water would not break. If it did, the baby would be born prematurely and had no chance of survival. Later that evening, in the middle of Canton Grace's communion service, Dan texted me. Kim's water broke. Our little grandson would be born and then pass away a few moments later since he was not sufficiently developed to survive. I had enough time to say a quick, silent prayer and then finish leading the communion service.

My dear mother passed away unexpectedly a year or so later. Without going into the details, she passed away on a Saturday morning. By God's grace, I preached the next day, leaving little time to mourn.

Virtually the same scenario played out recently when my dear friend, fellow elder, and brother in the Lord, Kim Franks, passed away suddenly. God gave me an extra day to recover. It was a Friday morning and I preached that Sunday.

I have learned the lesson to trust the Lord as soon as possible with my trials. I'm going to trust Him eventually anyhow. I might as well trust Him on the front end. "Cast your burden on the Lord, and He shall sustain you; He shall never permit the righteous to be moved" (Psalm 55:22).

Lesson #5 - Never Doubt In the Dark What God Has Made Clear in the Light

It is an exhilarating experience to have Almighty God give us clarity and direction when we desperately need His guidance. The steps are well known. We have a decision to make. We are unclear as to what is the best choice. We pray earnestly for God's guidance and direction. In His time, (through open doors of opportunity, desires placed in our heart, and confirmation from others) He grants us the guidance we need. Then circumstances enter into our lives which can cause us to doubt God's crystal clear guidance.

Abraham is an excellent example of this dynamic. In Genesis 12:7 we read, "Then the Lord appeared to Abram and said, "To your descendants I will give this land." And there he built an altar to the Lord, who had appeared to him." Abraham arrived in the Promised Land and God appeared to Abraham and revealed to him that this is the land that He will give to Abraham's descendants. Abraham stays there for a time and then circumstances pressured him. "Now there was a famine in the land, and Abram went down to Egypt to dwell there, for the famine was severe in the land," Genesis 12:10. After leaving the land that God had promised to Abraham and his descendants, Abraham lied, claiming that Sarah was his sister. This exposed her to great harm and would have led to disaster apart from the protective hand of God. Never doubt in the dark what God has made clear in the light.

Our eleven and one half years of ministry in Palmyra Grace Brethren Church were rewarding, fruitful, and enjoyable. I must confess that the last twenty-one months were extremely challenging. Through a series of events God clearly led me to move to Canton, Ohio with my family to pastor Canton Grace Brethren Church. It was difficult to leave our beloved church family in Palmyra, but it was clearly the right thing to do. That clarity became fuzzy at Canton Grace as a new set of challenges presented themselves. It took God three years to get things on the right track, and the ministry at Canton Grace has been marvelous. There were times during the first three years where I questioned whether I discerned God's will correctly. I had, and the less I questioned, the better off I was.

Lesson #6 - God's Trials are Tailor Made for You

One of the classic passages in Scripture about trials is James 1:2-4, "My brethren, count it all joy when you fall into various trials, knowing that the testing of your faith produces patience. But let patience have its perfect work, that you may be perfect and complete, lacking nothing." James begins by telling us that we should see trials as a blessing from God. In fact, we should consider our trials to be pure joy, triggering nothing but joy in our hearts. This is true for any brother or sister in the Lord. This is true for any and all negative circumstances that God permits in our lives. Why should we have this perspective? One reason is that God is testing my faith. God's intention is that we pass the test, proving the genuineness of our faith, and to purify our faith. This will give us greater confidence in God and His promises in the future. Another compelling reason that we should consider trials to be nothing but joy is that God is forming our character. If we hang in there and let perseverance to do its work, we will become well-rounded in our character. That is the God intended purpose in our trials. If we submit to the trial and persevere through it, God will use the trial to smooth out our rough edges. The naturally mild-mannered person will learn to confront when necessary. The naturally aggressive, goal-oriented person will become more gentle and understanding. God not only permits trials in our life, but He also tailors them to accomplish His goal of making us well-rounded, like Jesus.

The Lord is committed to the holiness of all who belong to Him through saving faith in Christ Jesus. As Paul so beautifully wrote in Romans 8:29, "For whom He foreknew, He also predestined to be conformed to the image of His Son, that He might be the firstborn among many brethren." God is passionately committed to making us more like Jesus.

I have shared how my accounting employer wanted me to change some numbers to save a client almost $100,000 in taxes. My employer held me in lower esteem after I took my stand. From that experience, I learned the importance of standing by Godly convictions. The trial also increased my compassion for people in the work world, increased my commitment to stick to my pastoral calling, and convinced me to never desire to go back into accounting. It was a trial that was tailor made for me.

Lesson #7 - God Is Always Several Steps Ahead of Us

It is impossible for us to fathom that God is never surprised by anything new, that He never learns anything new, and that He never increases His understanding of what has, is, or will happen. Therefore, God is always "several steps" ahead of us in every circumstance in life. This is especially comforting as we are going through trials.

In Mark 14, we read about the Lord preparing for the Jewish Passover, also known as the Last Supper. In verses 12-16, we read, "Now on the first day of Unleavened Bread, when they killed the Passover lamb, His disciples said to Him, 'Where do You want us to go and prepare, that You may eat the Passover?' And He sent out two of His disciples and said to them, 'Go into the city, and a man will meet you carrying a pitcher of water; follow him. Wherever he goes in, say to the master of the house, The Teacher says, where is the guest room in which I may eat the Passover with My disciples? ' Then he will show you a large upper room, furnished and prepared; there make ready for us.' So His disciples went out, and came into the city, and found it just as He had said to them; and they prepared the Passover." The Lord knew that a man would be carrying a pitcher of water, what time he would be carrying it, that he would go to his master's home, and that the master of the house would have a house that was perfect for the Passover meal.

God is several steps ahead of us. What seems to be a trial to us is merely an opportunity to trust in our all-knowing, totally in control, wise, and loving heavenly Father.

Tom Eames was an associate pastor at Canton Grace. He pastored the youth and led worship at the contemporary service. Tom announced that he was accepting a call to pastor a small church in Strongsville, Ohio. Who would lead worship at our contemporary service? A month before Tom announced his resignation, the Lord brought Geoff Swartz and his family to our church family. Geoff was an experienced and talented worship team leader. The Lord used a saying about serving the Lord that I had posted earlier to convict him that God wanted him to be our new worship team leader. With God, all bases are covered even when we can't foresee how He will cover them.

Lesson #8 - God Doesn't Enjoy Our Trials, But He Knows That We Need Them

When I was younger in my walk with the Lord, I used to think that God actually enjoyed watching me muddle my way through a trial. "Here I am suffering and You are enjoying the show," I would think. Nothing could be farther from the truth. God doesn't enjoy our afflictions any more than a good parent enjoys disciplining their children. In Isaiah 49:13 we read, "Sing, O heavens! Be joyful, O earth! And break out in singing, O mountains! For the Lord has comforted His people, and will have mercy on His afflicted." God does not enjoy chastising those who belong to Him. He knows what is best for us. He knows what will make us more like Jesus and He is passionately committed to that end.

I hope that you more fully appreciate God's grace as we navigate our way through the trials of life. The Lord desires for us to become better and never for us to become bitter. Let's humbly trust Him to pour out His grace as we accept all trials as coming from His kind and wise Hand.

Chapter 7 – God's Grace in Living for Jesus

God pours out an exceedingly large amount of grace when He reconciles us to Himself through faith in His Son Jesus. That initial burst of grace is followed by innumerable expressions of His grace as we live our lives to please Him. We have a tendency to think that once we are saved by God's grace, we can live the Christian life without divine assistance. Nothing could be further from the truth. Here are a few ways that we need God's gracious Hand to live for Jesus after we are saved.

When We are Weak Then We are Strong

One of the dichotomies of the Christian life is that we experience God's strength the most when we are most aware of our weakness. In fact, there are times when God arranges circumstances so that we are acutely aware that we are in over our head. Paul experienced this reality in his life on several occasions. In II Corinthians 1:8-10 Paul notes, "For we do not want you to be ignorant, brethren, of our trouble which came to us in Asia: that we were burdened beyond measure, above strength, so that we despaired even of life. Yes, we had the sentence of death in ourselves, that we should not trust in ourselves but in God who raises the dead, who delivered us from so great a death, and does deliver us; in whom we trust that He will still deliver us." Facing death, Paul and Timothy threw themselves totally upon the grace of God and experienced His saving power from the jaws of death.

When Paul was tormented by a thorn in the flesh, a messenger of Satan, he was forced to completely trust the Lord. The messenger, which was either a demon or an evil antagonist, was not removed from Paul's life by God in order to keep Paul humble and dependent upon Him. In II Corinthians 12:9 we read, "And He said to me, "My grace is sufficient for you, for my strength is made perfect in weakness. Therefore most gladly I will rather boast in my infirmities, that the power of Christ may rest upon me." The secret to experiencing God's power is to know that we desperately need His power and to ask Him for it.

Some of the most effective sermons that I have preached are when I am physically sick. Some of the best decisions I've made is when the decision is too difficult for me to figure out on my own. Some of the most remarkable answers to prayer have come in response to me admitting that I am in way over my head. The typical Christian progresses as followers: "I need you, Lord, when it is really hard. I need you, Lord, when it is hard. I need you, Lord, all the time."

In Order to Grow in Areas of Weakness

We all have areas of strength and weakness. Some weaknesses are particularly noticeable and difficult to overcome. We need God's grace over time to make progress. We are blessed to have a God who is committed to our holiness. In I Thessalonians 5:23-24 we read, "Now may the God of peace Himself sanctify you completely; and may your whole spirit, soul, and body be preserved blameless at the coming of our Lord Jesus Christ. He who calls you is faithful, who also will do it." "To sanctify" means to make holy. God is faithful to work on our holiness as we cooperate with Him. In Romans 8:29 we read, "For whom He foreknew, He also predestined to be conformed to the image of His Son, that He might be the firstborn among many brethren." Those people that are in a love relationship with God He also predetermined to make them more and more like His perfect Son, Jesus.

My experience and observation is that God is in no hurry to make us like Jesus. From the moment of our salvation until the day we pass away is the time He has to complete His work. My experience also has been to focus on Jesus and walking with Him. He then does the work of smoothing out my rough edges. If I try to make my weaknesses strong, I end up frustrated and ineffective. When I focus on Jesus, the Holy Spirit slowly makes me more like Him. In II Corinthians 3:18 Paul writes, "But we all, with unveiled face, beholding as in a mirror the glory of the Lord, are being transformed into the same image from glory to glory, just as by the Spirit of the Lord." God's grace makes us more like Jesus the more we study and look into the face of Jesus. We see Him especially in the New Testament which clearly depicts His life and flawless character.

While growing up in Pittsburgh, Pennsylvania, all members of my extended family knew my greatest character flaw. I was known for my hot, Italian temper. I especially didn't like to lose…at anything! When I did, everyone knew that I was not pleased. I don't know how many times I knocked the playroom sliding doors off their track in a fit of anger. The Lord worked in that area quickly after coming to Jesus. Over time I lost my temper less and less frequently. Our kids saw dad get angry while growing up, but infrequently enough that none of them has a temper problem. Over the years, I didn't "work on my temper." I read, memorized, studied, and listened to God's Word for tens of thousands of hours. I prayed and served Him. Jesus took care of the rest by His wonderful grace.

<u>Experiencing Real Success</u>

Everyone wants to be successful. Regardless of one's goals and aspirations, we all dream of doing well, of enjoying the thrill of victory. We can certainly focus on some key ingredients for success. Hard work, staying focused, and building a good team around us are all part of the recipe for success. However, apart from the grace of God, all the best efforts we can muster will end in disappointment.

This is especially true in serving the Lord. In I Corinthians 3:5-7 we read, "Who then is Paul, and who is Apollos, but ministers through whom you believed, as the Lord gave to each one? I planted, Apollos watered, but God gave the increase. So then neither he who plants is anything, nor he who waters, but God who gives the increase." God uses hard work, smart work, and efficient work to be sure. Without His work, it will all amount to nothing.

I've always been humbled as I think about the ministries of Jeremiah and Jonah. Jeremiah was a noble, faithful, and honorable man of God who saw little fruit for his exemplary efforts. Jonah, on the other hand, possessed none of the virtues named above. Instead he was stubborn, bigoted, and a very slow learner. He had the privilege of seeing countless people from Nineveh genuinely repent and avoid national judgement. We can only explain this perplexing reality by the sovereign grace of God. God chose to use Jonah in wonderful ways despite Jonah.

The same can be said about making money or building wealth. In I Chronicles 29:12 we read, "Both riches and honor come from You, And You reign over all. In Your hand is power and might; in Your hand it is to make great and to give strength to all." Why do some people make money effortlessly while others work hard to make ends meet? A large part of the answer is the sovereign plan and grace of God.

Solomon gives us the right perspective when it comes to building wealth. In Proverbs chapter 8 he describes wisdom personified. He writes in Proverbs 8:21, "That I may cause those who love me to inherit wealth, that I may fill their treasuries." In other words, work hard, apply your heart to gain wisdom, and let God bless you financially as He pleases. Success is tied, in every area of life, to God's grace.

Finding a Good Mate

So many things can go the wrong way when it comes to choosing a lifelong mate. Who doesn't put their best foot forward when they are dating someone they like? Then after marriage, the person shows their true colors. Furthermore, all of us change. Our spouses change. Some spousal changes can be unpleasant and unappealing. There are times when a spouse does not handle disappointments. These disappointments make life frustrating and annoying. Tight finances create undue stress, in-laws may be divisive, and the list goes on.

Perhaps the most humbling reasons that a marriage can be unhappy is our inability to properly evaluate people. We think the man or woman is a real catch. Unfortunately, love can be blind and we overlook the obvious.

All of this to say that finding a good mate requires the grace of God. We can tilt the odds in our favor, but only God knows the future. As Solomon wrote in Proverbs 19:14, "Houses and riches are an inheritance from fathers, but a prudent wife is from the Lord." We can safely say that a prudent husband is from the Lord as well.

How Long We Live. How Well We Feel.

Our culture is obsessed with the way we look, how healthy we eat, and the effectiveness of our exercise programs. We are convinced that we can extend our life by exercising properly, eating healthily, and staying away from alcohol and drugs. I practice all three of the above disciplines. I am especially fastidious when it comes to exercising. My weight lifting routine was, for many years, a bit overdone. One of my nicknames was "The Pumping Pastor." One of the young people in church would joke that I not only would preach the Bible, but at the end of the sermon I would rip it apart. Hyperbole, but you get the point. The combination of exercise, eating well, and abstaining from substances that harm the body are common sense practices. They will improve the quality of anyone's life, but not the quantity of one's days. In Job 14:5, we read, "Since his days *are* determined, the number of his months *is* with You; you have appointed his limits, so that he cannot pass." The number of everyone's days is determined. That means that God ordains the number of days we will live. That is different than merely knowing the number of our days. God also has appointed our limits. We cannot go pass our predetermined expiration date.

God does tend to bless, as a rule of thumb, godly living. In Proverbs 3:1-2 Solomon writes, "My son, do not forget my law, but let your heart keep my commands; for length of days and long life and peace they will add to you." Obeying the Lord and the wise counsel of parents is something that God tends to bless. Some very godly people do not live long lives. Proverbs 3:1-2 is a proverb, a proverbial saying that is true, but it is not a promise. Some wonderful brothers and sisters in the Lord pass away in their fifties or sixties. What determines the length of our days and the health of those days? Ultimately, it is the goodness and grace of God.

<u>Grace to Forgive and to Be Forgiven</u>

A necessary part of the human experience is forgiveness. We all offend and are offended. We expect to be forgiven, but we find it hard to forgive. Forgiveness is an act of grace. No one earns forgiveness. It is extended freely by the one who forgives. In fact, one of the New Testament Greek words for forgiveness has the word "grace" in its root. In Ephesians 4:32 Paul writes," And be kind to one another, tenderhearted, forgiving one another, even as God in Christ forgave you." We are to forgive as we have been forgiven by God the Father through the sacrifice of Jesus for us. We are forgiven by grace. We forgive others by extending grace.

Extending grace benefits the person that we forgive. It benefits us to an even greater extent. The poison of an unforgiving heart is a huge burden. Hebrews 12:15 states, "looking carefully lest anyone fall short of the grace of God; lest any root of bitterness springing up cause trouble, and by this many become defiled." An unforgiving heart leads to bitterness. Bitterness causes trouble for the person with the bitter heart and for those who interact with him.

Like everyone, I have strengths and weaknesses. Forgiving others would be a strength of mine. I have been forgiven much so forgiving generally is not a problem. There has been one significant exception. I really struggled to forgive a few people whose bad behavior forced me to leave a ministry that I really loved. My family had to be uprooted. Questions had to be answered. How could people be so cruel? How could God permit such evil? How will this impact my wife and kids? I had convinced myself that I had forgiven the guilty parties. I had not. Our hearts are deceitful, and we can trick ourselves without know it. My joy was sporadic, my heart was heavy, and my ministry had minimal power until I truly forgave others from my heart.

How did I forgive those who had caused my family and me considerable pain? It was an outpouring of God's grace. As I read a book about how to protect yourself from misbehaving lay people and how to recover as a pastor, I came across a couple of pages on forgiveness. As I read about the freedom and joy of forgiving those who have deeply hurt us, I yielded my heart to the Lord and what was written. I experienced a flood of peace in my heart. I was set free from the bondage of an unforgiving heart.

Forgiveness can also become a way of life. When it becomes part of who we are, people will ask us for forgiveness for things that really never bothered us or only bothered us momentarily. When we lived in Eastlake, Ohio, a suburb of Cleveland, we owned a little Toyota. It wasn't much to look at, but it ran beautifully. The only thing that didn't function well was the gas gauge. In fact, it didn't work at all. I kept track of the miles that I drove since I last filled the tank. I would then fill the tank up when I estimated that it was close to empty. This worked well for about a year. Then one evening, I miscalculated and we ran out of gas. The timing was less than ideal. It was at night, pitch black, and we ran out of gas on a busy interstate, interstate 271. I had a wife and three small children in the car with me. So I rolled up the windows, locked the car, and walked about one mile to the nearest exit and gas station. The employee had mercy on me. After paying for the gas, he drove me back to our car. I poured some gas into the tank. Remarkably, Melinda never made me feel any worse than I already felt. I don't even remember talking much about it. When forgiveness is a way of life, we forgive as an almost reflex reaction to the offenses of life. I should add that we did not own the car less than a year later.

If you are struggling to forgive someone, ask God to give you the grace to forgive. Mediate upon how much you have been forgiven. Ask God to help you to forgive as you have been forgiven. It takes an act of God's grace for us to have the grace to forgive others.

Finding Favor with Others

Isn't it wonderful when other people like us? We aren't sure why, and we know that it's not because we are trying to gain their favor. We are just being ourselves and they like us. This is a manifestation of God's grace.

When we find favor in someone else's eyes, it can be used by God in a number of wonderful ways. Young Daniel was being forced to eat King Nebuchadnezzar's food and to drink the king's wine. Both would compel him to violate the Old Testament law. What could Daniel do? In Daniel 1:9 we read, "Now God had brought Daniel into the favor and goodwill of the chief of the eunuchs." This favor gave Daniel and his three friends the opportunity to eat vegetables and drink water for ten days. This ten day test was honored by God as they appeared to be healthier than all the other young men who ate the king's food and drank his wine. Daniel and his three friends were protected by God from violating the Word of God.

When Joseph was unfairly slandered and thrown in prison, he enjoyed God-given favor. We read, "but the Lord was with Joseph and showed him mercy, and He gave him favor in the sight of the keeper of the prison," Genesis 39:21. The keeper of the prison put Joseph in charge of all the prisoners during his imprisonment.

I certainly have been the recipient of God's grace in ministry. Some of the best known pastors in the Charis Fellowship took a liking to me as a young man, invested in me, and helped me in numerous ways, including recommending me for pastoral positions. I love to recommend people for jobs, to give references for college, and to introduce people to others who may become their plumber, dentist, electrician, home repair man, or a host of other things.

We all need other people to succeed. I would never be who I am or have accomplished what I have accomplished without the help of other people. People who like me, have helped me, counseled me, invested in me, and believed in me have been invaluable in my life. We all need to gain favor in other people's lives. Such favor is a magnificent embodiment of the grace of God.

People Who Pray For Us

Most followers of the Lord Jesus will pray for themselves. They are concerned about a multitude of personal needs and lift them up to the Lord. Most believers also pray for their families. Our wife, husband, and kids are near and dear to our hearts. If the one time that a person prays is on their commute to work, you can be sure that they will pray for their personal needs and the needs of their family.

When a person prays for you, that is a work of the Holy Spirit in their life. We pray for people and circumstances that are on our heart. If you are on a person's heart, God has placed you there. It is a work of His grace on your behalf. In Zechariah 12:9-10, Zechariah writes, "And I will pour on the house of David and on the inhabitants of Jerusalem the Spirit of grace and supplication; then they will look on Me whom they pierced. Yes, they will mourn for Him as one mourns for his only son, and grieve for Him as one grieves for a firstborn." When Jesus returns to save the nation of Israel from their enemies at His second coming, God will pour out grace upon the Jewish people, giving them a heart to pray and intercede. Zechariah refers to it as a "Spirit of grace and supplication."

Our oldest son, Dan, was engaged to be married. In fact, he was less than a month and one half away from the altar. We knew that his fiancée was not ready for marriage, and we had serious doubts as to whether she was right for Dan. I talked to Dan expressing my concerns. It appeared that there was no way to stop the wedding from taking place. Burdened deeply, I prayed and fasted on a Thursday and my wife, Melinda, did the same. On Sunday evening, the wedding was called off and the relationship was over. A deep desire to pray for others is a work of the Holy Spirit and a work of His grace.

I am blessed to have a group of men who pray with me twice a month. They are called, "The Pastor's Prayer Team." I can only imagine the positive impact they have had in my life, the life of Canton Grace Church, and the lives of others. Melinda prays with a group of ladies before church on Wednesday evenings. They pray largely for family needs and have seen God's Hand at work on numerous occasions.

I thank God for praying friends, especially in the Lake County, Palmyra, and Canton Grace Brethren Churches. Their heartfelt prayers have helped me to serve, lead, and live for Jesus. They are a gift of God's grace to me.

<u>When There Is No Explanation but God</u>

God's grace is most clearly visible when there is no other way to explain what happened than to say "that must be the Hand of God." Times like these can cause our jaw to drop, our heart to leap, and our soul to be thrilled. Events like these are not a daily occurrence, but we remember them for many years.

Paul describes these inexplicable acts of divine grace, "Now to Him who is able to do exceedingly abundantly above all that we ask or think, according to the power that works in us, to Him be glory in the church by Christ Jesus to all generations, forever and ever. Amen," Ephesians 3:20-21. Jeremiah says it this way, "Call to Me, and I will answer you, and show you great and mighty things, which you do not know" (Jeremiah 33:3). Those who have eyes that can see attribute such marvelous works to the grace of God.

Recently I was asked to officiate the funeral service of a very dear sister in the Lord, Nancy Stoner. Nancy was as sweet a person that I have ever met. Her husband, Lowell, her daughter, and brother came in to plan the memorial service. When it came time to choose the hymns for the service, I mentioned that "In the Garden" was probably her favorite hymn. They agreed. Her daughter suggested "Amazing Grace." I said, "Certainly, that's a classic." No one had a suggestion for a third hymn. I advised that we should sing the third hymn after the devotional. I was planning to work on the devotional the following day. Perhaps I can choose a closing hymn that fits the devotional. They all agreed. The next day I chose a hymn, but I had no peace in my heart. So I chose another hymn, "Because He Lives," that tied into the message beautifully. The next day about forty-five minutes before the memorial service, Nancy's daughter mentioned that they had reviewed some information that Nancy had filled out six years earlier with the funeral home. At the bottom of the last page she scribbled that she wanted "Because He Lives," sung at her funeral! I couldn't believe it. There are over 500 hymns in Canton Grace's hymn book, and I chose the right one. It can only be explained by the grace and guidance of God. I should add that I was the song leader for the service. When it came time to lead the congregation in the final hymn, I said, "Please turn to hymn number 213, Because He Lives." I opened the hymnal and turned directly to hymn number 213. Only the Lord could have orchestrated the whole thing.

God loves to put His glory on display. What better time than when He intervenes and performs the impossible. Wayward adult kids come back to the Lord, impossible problems get solved, and hard-hearted friends and loved ones come to Christ. A wonderful aspect of being a Christian is praying and seeing God do only what God can do as an expression of His mercy and grace.

Conclusion - Grateful For Eternity

I hope that surveying these seven major areas of life have demonstrated that we need God's grace in every area of life. We are responsible to do our part, but we are in desperate need for Him to do His.

God's grace is truly amazing. When those who have trusted in Jesus' death on the cross to pay for all of their sins are residing in heaven, they will still be astounded by His infinite grace. In Ephesians 2:5-7 Paul writes, "Even when we were dead in trespasses, (God) made us alive together with Christ (by grace you have been saved), and raised us up together, and made us sit together in the heavenly places in Christ Jesus, <u>that in the ages to come He might show the exceeding riches of His grace in His kindness toward us in Christ Jesus.</u>"

I think John Newton captured it well in his famous hymn, "Amazing Grace." "When we've been there ten thousand years, bright shining as the sun, we've no less days to sing God's praise than when we'd first begun."

Since we will praise and give thanks to God for His grace for all eternity, we may as well start right now. May meditating upon His grace melt your heart, purify your soul, and motivate your will to live for Him.

It's All Grace.

Discussion Questions
<u>Chapter 1 - God's Grace in Growing Up</u>

1. In what ways has your parents' background formed and shaped you in positive ways?

2. How did your parents' guidance and wisdom help you discern your talents and passions?

3. Share an example of how God protected you physically, emotionally, or spiritually while growing up?

4. In what ways are you grateful for God's Hand in forming you in your mother's womb?

Chapter 2 - God's Grace in Salvation

1. How should we respond to the fact that God chose us to belong to Him for eternity? In what circumstances is this truth especially helpful?

2. What people did God bring into your life that helped you give your life to Jesus? Describe the influence they had.

3. What hardships did God use to get your attention and soften your heart towards Him?

4. What are some ways that God can use our personal testimony?

Chapter 3 - God's Grace in Marriage

1. What are some non-negotiable qualities to look for in a husband or a wife? What are some qualities that are negotiable?

2. Why is it important to wait on the Lord, and what are some pitfalls of moving forward without His direction? What are some things to help a single person wait?

3. What are some ways for a husband to love his wife? What are some ways for a wife to help her husband?

4. What are some of the main dynamics that make God's grace essential for a joyful marriage?

Chapter 4 - God's Grace in Raising a Family

1. What are some benefits to having children?

2. What are some specific ways to love your children?

3. What are some challenges of teaching your kids the Bible? How can we make sure that our life does not undermine what we teach?

4. What are some of the most important things to keep in mind when relating to your kids as they grow older?

Chapter 5 - God's Grace in Fulfilling Your Calling

1. How did God guide you into your calling? Tell your story. Where do you see God's Hand?

2. What are some things that you have done or thought to help you when work is difficult?

3. What are some signs that God is moving you to another job or a completely different calling?

4. What fruit have you seen in your work? Do you thank God when you see fruit?

Chapter 6 - God's Grace in the Midst of Trials

1. Which of the eight lessons in this chapter did you find most helpful? Why?

2. Share a recent trial. How is it tailor-made for you?

3. What are some reasons that we should trust God as soon as possible for the trial?

4. What are some thoughts that can help us accept trials as coming from God's good hand?

Chapter 7 - God's Grace in Living for Jesus

1. How do you measure real success? In what ways does God give us success at work, in our homes, as a follower of Jesus?

2. What makes forgiveness hard? What are some things that help you forgive others?

3. Share an experience where God gave you favor with someone and how it benefitted you.

4. Share a story of how God answered a prayer in a wonderful way. Thank Him for His grace.

ABOUT THE AUTHOR

From 1988-present, Joe Cosentino has served in three Charis
Fellowship Churches, Lake County Grace Church, Palmyra Grace
Church, and Canton Grace Church. He earned his Master of Divinity
degree from Grace Seminary.

In 1982 he married the love of his life, Melinda, and together they
have served the Lord with their four adult children, Dan, Marianne,
Tony, and Joe Jr. They have two granddaughters, Charis and Callie.